ACTION SCIENCE

THE SCIENCE OF A

RACE CAR

REACTIONS IN ACTION

by Heather E. Schwartz

Consultant:
Paul Ohmann, PhD
Associate Professor of Physics
University of St. Thomas, St. Paul, Minnesota

CAPSTONE PRESS
a capstone imprint

Fact Finders is published by Capstone Press,
151 Good Counsel Drive, P.O. Box 669, Mankato, Minnesota 56002.
www.capstonepress.com

092009
005620LKS10

Books published by Capstone Press are manufactured with paper
containing at least 10 percent post-consumer waste.

Library of Congress Cataloging-in-Publication Data
Schwartz, Heather E.
   The science of a race car: reactions in action / by Heather E. Schwartz
   p. cm. — (Fact finders. Action science)
   Summary: "Describes the science behind race cars, including aerodynamics, velocity, and fuel
types" — Provided by publisher.
   Includes bibliographical references and index.
   ISBN 978-1-4296-3955-2 (library binding)
   ISBN 978-1-4296-4855-4 (paperback)
   1. Automobiles, Racing — Juvenile literature. 2. Aerodynamics — Juvenile literature. 3. Friction — Juvenile
literature. 4. Speed — Juvenile literature. I. Title. II. Series.
TL236.S37 2010
629.228 — dc22   2009033241

Editorial Credits
Lori Shores, editor; Lori Bye, designer; Jo Miller, media researcher; Eric Manske, production specialist

Photo Credits
AP Images/Larry Papke, 11
Dreamstime/Actionsports/Walter Arce, 7, 27; Sideline, 6
Getty Images for NASCAR/Chris McGrath, 12; Jason Smith, cover; Jerry Markland, 25; John Harrelson, 18, 20;
    Rusty Jarrett, 8, 28
Getty Images Inc./Chris Graythen, 5; Ezra Shaw, 19; Jamie Squire, 26; John Harrelson, 15, 16, 17, 23;
    Todd Warshaw, 9, 10
Shutterstock/First Class Photos PTY LTD, 29 (bottom); Goxy, 3 (design element); Sebastian Kaulitzki, 29 (top)

Essential content terms are **bold** and are defined at the bottom of the page where they first appear.

TABLE OF CONTENTS

SCIENCE IN MOTION

Imagine getting behind the wheel of a **stock car** and taking off around the track. The engine would roar. The tires would squeal and smoke. Some surprising things would happen too. You'd experience firsthand how forces of science work on a race car.

Fans don't need to know the science behind race cars to enjoy amazing wins or sudden spinouts. But science can explain every action and reaction on the track. Race car drivers put science to work as they struggle to reach the finish line first. During every race, they prove science is more than a subject to study in school. On the track, science can cause one car to crash while another pulls ahead for the win.

stock car — a car built for racing that is based on the regular model sold to the public

4

CHAPTER 1

START YOUR ENGINES!

A race car speeds through a qualifying lap two days before a big race. The car slips through the air easily thanks to its sleek body design. Race cars sit low to the ground so more air passes over the car. The air rushing over the top creates **downforce**. During high-speed turns, downforce keeps the car on the track instead of flying out of control. In a crash, flaps on the roof flip up to push more air to the top of the car. Even if the car spins, the extra air pressure keeps it on the ground.

---

downforce — the force of passing air pressing down on a moving vehicle

airflow

Front air dam directs air up and over car.

Spoiler pushes air down over rear of car.

Race car safety belts are stronger than seat belts in ordinary cars.

ON YOUR MARK

The driver earned a good starting position based on the qualifying lap. As the driver heads to the front of the lineup, Newton's first law of motion comes to mind. This law says an object in motion will stay in motion unless an outside force acts upon it. In a crash, the car stops, but the driver keeps moving until stopped by the windshield. The driver tightens the safety belts, just in case.

SEE FOR YOURSELF

Use chalk to draw a line on the sidewalk. Step back 10 feet (3 meters) and run. Try to stop right on the line. Even if you can stop your feet, your chest and arms will keep moving forward. It's not easy to stop once you're in motion.

GET SET

Race car engines rev and rumble while drivers wait for the race to start. The action has already begun, even though the fans can't see it. Thousands of explosions are taking place inside each car's internal combustion engine. When the drivers started their cars, they set metal rods called pistons in motion. The pistons slide up and down in tubes filled with a mixture of air and gasoline. Every time the pistons go up, they create a spark. The mixture reacts by exploding. The explosions create the energy needed to move the car.

Engines rumble as race cars line up for the race.

Race car mechanics are always working to improve the performance of race car engines.

Regular cars run on internal combustion engines too. But race car engines are built for power and speed. The pistons of a race car engine are bigger and slide in shorter tubes. These pistons create more power faster than regular cars. Regular car engines produce about 200 **horsepower**. But stock car engines produce about 750 horsepower. Other race cars, such as Top Fuel dragsters, have engines that produce about 7,000 horsepower.

horsepower — a unit for measuring the power of engines and motors

The green flag signals the start of the race. It is also used throughout the race to show drivers that track conditions are good.

GO!

A green flag drops, and the fans start screaming. The race is on! As the car rushes forward, the driver is reminded of Newton's first law of motion again. Another part of Newton's law says an object at rest will stay at rest unless acted upon by an outside force. As the car **accelerates**, the driver's seat moves forward with the car. But the driver's body stays in place until forced into action. In a race car, the lightning-fast acceleration pushes the driver back in the seat.

accelerate — to gain speed

McDowell Survives Crash!

In 2008, NASCAR driver Michael McDowell lost control of his car during a qualifying lap at Texas Motor Speedway. The car slammed into a sidewall at 170 miles (274 kilometers) per hour. The car flipped and rolled over several times before bursting into flames. Thanks to the science of safety belts and fire-resistant clothing, McDowell walked away from the crash. His only injuries were a few bruises.

Tires squeal and smoke, and fans get a whiff of burning rubber. The tires moving on the track cause **friction**. As the two surfaces rub together, friction helps the tires grip the track. Friction also causes the sounds and smells.

friction

Friction produces heat, which increases the air pressure in tires. Higher pressure makes air expand, or take up more space. If the tires expand too much during a race, the driver will have trouble. The car might slide, skid, spin out, or even crash. To avoid these problems, many race car tires are filled with dry nitrogen instead of air. Dry nitrogen doesn't expand and contract as much with changes in temperature.

friction — the force produced when two objects rub against each other

SEE FOR YOURSELF

You can use a balloon to see air contract and expand. Fill a balloon with air and put it in the freezer for one hour. After an hour, the balloon will no longer look full. The air in the balloon contracted as it cooled. When the balloon warms up, the air will expand again. The balloon will look full again.

CHAPTER 2

ON TRACK

Air in front of the car creates drag.

Heading down the track, the race cars form a line, riding almost bumper to bumper. The drivers know that race cars speed faster when **drafting** than they do alone. Drafting lowers the amount of **drag** that is created when a car moves through air. Drag is created by air pushing against a moving object. In a draft, the lead car does most of the work. It cuts through the air at the front of the line. The cars behind the lead car don't have to work as hard to push through the air. At high speeds, drafting also creates a flow of air that pushes the lead car forward even faster.

draft — to drive very closely behind another vehicle to reduce drag

drag — the force that holds an object back as it moves through air

Second car doesn't have to cut through the air.

Disturbed airflow at rear of car creates drag.

SEE FOR YOURSELF

An object with less surface area moves through air more easily than one with a large surface area. Test this idea with two sheets of scrap paper. Crumple one in a ball. Hold both sheets over your head, one in each hand, and drop them at the same time. The crumpled sheet falls faster because it has less surface being pushed by the air.

COLLISION COURSE

Gripping the steering wheel, one driver looks for a way to pass the car ahead. The driver prepares to pull out of the draft but gets too close to the car ahead. The flow of air is disturbed, causing the front car to lose **traction**. The car's back end slips side to side, and the car starts to spin out.

traction — the gripping power that keeps a moving object from slipping on a surface

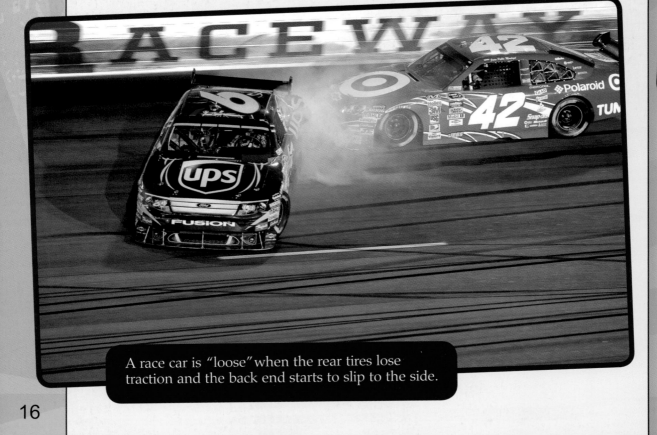

A race car is "loose" when the rear tires lose traction and the back end starts to slip to the side.

The driver stomps on the brakes to slow down,
but the car doesn't stop. Just as Newton's first law
says, the car stays in motion. The front brakes lock,
and the tires skid along the track. The driver tries
to turn, but the car doesn't have enough traction.
The car crashes into another car. Pieces of metal
fly through the air as both cars spin out of control.

The other drivers can't avoid the mess left on the track by the crash. Dirt and **debris** get stuck in the grille on the front of one car. With the grille clogged, air can't get through to cool the engine. The driver makes a pit stop, knowing that a clogged grille could cause the engine to overheat.

Multiple-car crashes create a lot of smoke and debris on the track.

Members of the pit crew work fast to refuel the race car, change tires, and make other repairs.

The engine isn't the only thing that gets hot in a race car. When the excitement heats up, so does the inside of the race car. The temperature inside the car can reach 150 degrees Fahrenheit (66 degrees Celsius). The driver has actually lost weight from sweating so much.

The driver tightens the safety belts while waiting for the pit crew to finish. The crew fills the gas tank, cleans the grille, and changes the tires. Working together, the pit crew has the car ready to race again in 14 seconds flat.

---

debris — the scattered pieces of something that has been broken or destroyed

FIRE!

An out-of-control race car flips and smashes into the sidewall. The car skids along the track on its side. Friction between the car and the track creates sparks as gas leaks from the fuel tank. Suddenly the car bursts into flames. Firefighters react quickly and rush to the scene.

A crash can cause fuel to leak from the gas tank. Friction caused this car to burst into flames after hitting another car.

Not all race cars use the same type of fuel. Stock car engines burn 110-octane gasoline, which provides more power than the gasoline used in regular cars. Top Fuel dragsters use a liquid explosive that is dangerous to handle. Used as fuel, the explosive chemical creates more power than gasoline. Methanol, used in Indy cars, is a type of alcohol that doesn't catch fire as easily as gasoline. And if it does catch fire, the flames can be put out with water. Firefighters need special foams to put out chemical and gasoline fires.

Mears on Fire!

Rick Mears was in the lead during the 1981 Indianapolis 500 when things went terribly wrong. When his car was refueled during a pit stop, 5 gallons (19 liters) of methanol spilled onto Mears. Less than a second later, he was on fire. Since methanol flames are nearly invisible, the firefighters didn't realize he needed help. Mears was saved by his fireproof suit and his father, who saw him slapping at the flames.

CHAPTER 3

REACHING THE FINISH LINE

A rookie driver presses hard on the gas pedal, racing at top speed through each lap. The engine gets hotter and hotter. The heat causes the aluminum parts of the engine to bend. Liquids boil and expand, threatening to burst hoses. Still the driver speeds ahead.

The heat from friction between the tires and the racetrack is also causing problems. The heat weakens the rubber, so the tires wear out more quickly. The car makes a turn, but the friction is too much for the tires. One of them blows, sending the car skidding out of control.

Experienced drivers know speeding as fast as possible isn't always a smart idea. Slowing down, especially during turns, gives the engine and tires a break. Some drivers take several laps at a slower speed. They don't use their top speed until the race is nearly over.

The blown tire isn't this car's only problem. Damage to a race car's body changes airflow around the car and increases drag.

SEE FOR YOURSELF

You can create friction with your hands. First, feel how warm your hands are by putting them on your cheeks. Then quickly rub your hands together for 10 seconds. Touch them to your cheeks again, and you'll notice they feel warmer.

THE LAST LAP

Cheering fans yell louder as the race cars speed around the track for the last few laps. The drivers have been working together in a draft. But now, each one wants to win.

One driver moves closer to the car ahead and bumps it. The move pushes the car forward giving the driver space to pass. The driver pulls out of the draft with another car following close behind. The airflow from the car in front and the car behind is an advantage. The middle car is pulled and pushed forward at the same time.

The driver feels confident as the car makes the last turn. The driver accelerates, and comes out of the turn without losing speed. The car moves to the front of the pack! The driver floors it down the straightaway and passes the car in first place. The driver speeds across the finish line and spots the checkered flag. Victory!

CHAPTER 4

YOU NEVER KNOW

Understanding science helps race car drivers on the track. But science can't guarantee a win. Race conditions can change in an instant. A minor crash could damage a car's body, changing airflow and creating drag. On a hot day, drivers can become sick if they don't drink enough water. A change in the weather could make the track conditions worse or better. And a mistake made by one driver can affect other drivers on the track.

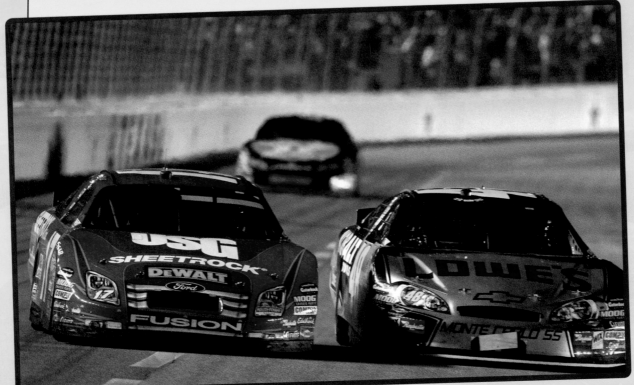

It might feel good to be in the lead, but race car drivers know anything can happen in a fraction of a second.

You never know what will happen in a race. Drivers think fast and make split-second decisions. Crew members determine what the car needs based on everything happening on the track. In a way, they're all acting like scientists. They watch carefully, think creatively, and experiment with new ways to win.

RACING FACTS

• In 1895, the first American car race took place on slippery dirt roads covered with fresh snow. Winner Frank Duryea's fastest speed was just 7.5 miles (12 kilometers) per hour.

• The fastest lap speed in a stock car is 212.809 miles (342.483 kilometers) per hour. Driver Bill Elliott holds the record for his driving at Talladega Superspeedway in 1987.

• Pit crews practice stops to be as fast as possible. A coach times them and videotapes their work. Fast crews can win thousands of dollars in pit stop competitions.

pit crew competition

•Top Fuel dragsters can accelerate from 0 to 100 miles (161 kilometers) per hour in less than one second.

OTHER SCIENCES IN ACTION

The Human Brain — Race car drivers need strong mental focus. Excitement floods drivers' brains with hormones. The hormones create a burst of energy to help the drivers stay alert.

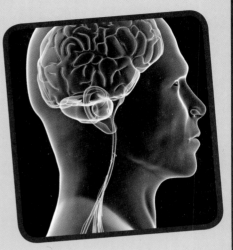

Physical Strength — It isn't easy to control a race car going 180 miles (290 kilometers) per hour. Drivers need strong muscles to handle race cars for three to four hours without breaks.

Safety Features — A roll cage made of steel tubing and padding protects the driver. If a race car lands upside down or on its side, the roll cage stops the car and the driver from getting crushed.

roll cage

Glossary

accelerate (ak-SEH-luh-rayt) — to gain speed

debris (duh-BREE) — the scattered pieces of something that has been broken or destroyed

downforce (DOUN-fors) — the force of passing air pressing down on a moving vehicle

draft (DRAFT) — to drive very closely behind another vehicle to reduce drag

drag (DRAG) — the force created when air strikes a moving object; drag slows down moving objects.

friction (FRIK-shuhn) — the force produced when two objects rub against each other; friction slows down moving objects.

horsepower (HORSS-pow-ur) — a unit for measuring an engine's power; one horsepower is the energy needed to move 550 pounds (249 kilograms) over a distance of 1 foot (30 centimeters) in one second.

stock car (STOK CAR) — a car built for racing that is based on the regular model sold to the public; NASCAR uses stock cars.

traction (TRAK-shuhn) — the gripping power that keeps a moving object from slipping on a surface

Read More

Abramson, Andra Serlin. *Race Cars Up Close.* New York: Sterling, 2008.

Hammond, Richard. *Car Science.* New York: DK, 2008.

Hofer, Charles. *Race Cars.* World's Fastest Machines. New York: PowerKids Press, 2008.

Internet Sites

FactHound offers a safe, fun way to find Internet sites related to this book. All of the sites on FactHound have been researched by our staff.

Here's all you do:

Visit *www.facthound.com*

FactHound will fetch the best sites for you!

Index